Discovering
Church
Architecture

SHIRE PUBLICATIONS LTD

Contents

Illustrations by the author.
The cover photograph of the parish church, Northleach, Gloucestershire, is by Cadbury Lamb.

Published in 2000 by Shire Publications Ltd, Cromwell House, Church Street, Princes Risborough, Buckinghamshire HP27 9AA, UK. Website: www.shirebooks.co.uk
Copyright © 1976 by Mark Child. First published 1976; reprinted 1979, 1984, 1987, 1992, 1996 and 2000. Number 214 in the Discovering series. ISBN 0 85263 328 9.

Printed in Great Britain by CIT Printing Services Ltd, Press Buildings, Merlins Bridge, Haverfordwest, Pembrokeshire SA61 1XF.

Introduction

Down by the chancel arch, the verger is mildly enthusiastic about the 'fine stiff leaf below the abacus on the respond'. The little group of people by him look nervously in the direction of his perfunctory wave. But now he is mentioning that the chancel arch has 'impost and plinth and chamfered edges similar to the respond in the south arcade'. An unspoken plea loudly pervades the heady atmosphere of the centuries, as it does throughout the length and breadth of the country: 'What on earth is he talking about?' If the truth be known, the visitors — mentally speaking — left their guide way back at the south porch. There he said: 'Behind us is a square-headed doorway with four-centred arch opening, carved spandrels and label stop'. Yet the little group perseveres, dogging the verger's footsteps, trying to justify his naive faith in their knowledge of church architecture.

Here is a tourist industry which is on the increase. Relatively new as a popular pastime, it has been for so long almost exclusive to architects and ecclesiastics. The result is that — in so many cases — the parson, the verger and the guide are finding it so difficult to communicate their expert knowledge to the layman visitor. And the visitor is left to look wildly about him or shuffle vaguely, if hopefully, through the pages of his guide book. The aim of this glossary is to help out everyone. It describes each term and every feature one is likely to encounter in a parish church and illustrates a great number of them. Above all, it should help to break down this particular communications barrier — and, it is hoped, increase the visitor's understanding and enjoyment.

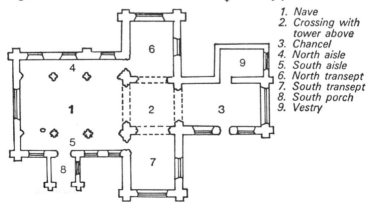

1. Nave
2. Crossing with tower above
3. Chancel
4. North aisle
5. South aisle
6. North transept
7. South transept
8. South porch
9. Vestry

GROUND PLAN OF A LARGE COUNTRY CHURCH

Guide books

You may be a habitual church visitor, a special features admirer, or just in out of the rain. Perhaps you just like to sit in the peace and quiet, or smell the mixture of flowers, mustiness and metal polish. Whatever your reason you should know that you are in a building which is architecturally unique. No two churches are alike and almost all have a feature or variation which you are unlikely ever to see elsewhere. All of this may not be apparent to the unpractised eye and for this reason I would add a plea in favour of the guide book, if one exists.

A pile of leaflets on the font, the table by the south door or the bookstall means that someone has taken the trouble to provide a guide for visitors. They will often have been written with the loving care of someone long associated with the church and printed at his own expense. Some are badly written and inadequately printed; some are professionally produced. But every one you buy will serve as a record of your own visit, and your few pence will help to keep the fabric intact for others who will come after you.

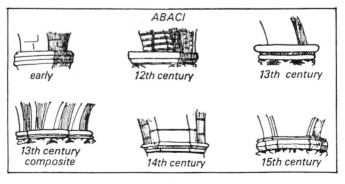

ABACI

early

12th century

13th century

13th century composite

14th century

15th century

A dictionary of church architecture

Abacus
Flat slab of stone which forms the uppermost member of a capital. It is set between the lintel and the column below as a supporting stone and positioned to take the concentrated weight at the point from which an arch springs. Abaci may be square, round or octagonal.

Abbey
Ecclesiastical dwelling, church, etc, for the use of nuns or monks and presided over by an abbess or abbot. In the Middle Ages they acquired vast quantities of land which they worked and farmed themselves. Between 1536 and 1540 Henry VIII destroyed almost all of them, appropriated their land for the Crown and sold it.

Abutment

Abutment
Pillar or buttress of solid masonry which is essentially part of an arch which springs from it. Its purpose is to withstand the sideways stress imposed by the arch.

Acanthus leaf
Decorative leaf-form which was sculptured on Corinthian capitals, although a more fleshy version is widely used on other types.

Acanthus leaf

Acoustic jars
Earthenware pots which were placed in various positions around the church in order to improve the sound.

Aisle
Section of the church parallel and adjacent to one or both sides of the nave. Aisles usually run the full length of the nave and are separated from it by a row of arches.

Alms box

Almery see Aumbry

Alms box
Receptacle used to collect the offerings of the people in the parish towards any number of causes. These ranged from the large amounts of money needed to finance the Crusades to smaller donations for the poor.

Altar
Flat-topped wooden or stone table, usually at the east end of the chancel, and raised above the level of the

Altar canopy

church. It contains the cross and other objects of importance.

Altar canopy
Decorated ceiling either suspended over (as a tester) or directly above the altar. The idea is simply to draw especial attention to the important feature below.

Altar frontal

Altar frontal
Richly decorated material which covers the front of the altar. The main colour in the cloth is changed in accordance with the liturgical colour associated with each season of the church's year.

Altar rails

Altar rails
Wooden or iron structure with gates, usually across the chancel in front of the altar. Sometimes the rails enclose the altar on three or four sides. They date from Elizabethan times and became popular in the seventeenth century as an alternative to chancel screens.

Altar stone
Flat stone slab which formed the top of a pre-Reformation altar. It was sometimes incised or marked with five consecration crosses — one in the centre, and another at each of the four corners.

Ambulatory
Used loosely to describe any walkway such as an aisle, arcade or cloisters. More properly the aisle or processional pathway behind the high altar, or the semicircular or polygonal passage to a chapel beyond the wall of the church at the east. end. They are usually bounded by an arcade or colonnade.

Ambulatory

Anchorite cell
Small dwelling in which a pious person passed her (the majority of them were women) days in solitary confinement. Such cells were usually built against the northern exterior of the church. The anchorite was able to see the high altar through a hole in the wall, and there was another in the outside wall to allow food to be passed in by the local people.

Angle buttresses

Angle buttress
Supporting masonry so constructed at the corner of a building that it exactly meets a similar structure built at a right angle to itself.

Anglo-Saxon see Saxon

Annulet

Annulet
Small, narrow ring of stone or metal around a circular pillar or detached shaft. A feature of Romanesque and Gothic building.

Apse
Semicircular or polygonal end to the chancel, or as an extension to a transept. The term is also used to describe a similarly shaped chapel extending anywhere beyond the walls of the main body of the church, but usually at the eastern end. Apses are often vaulted.

Apsidal see Apse

Apse

Arcade
Range of arches — usually separating the nave from the aisles — supported on pillars or columns. They may be open or closed (blind arcade), used to strengthen a wall or simply decorate it. Arcades may also support clerestory walls which form the roof of an adjacent aisle.

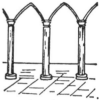

Arcade

Arcading
Technically as arcade. However, this term tends to be applied more to the use of a series of arches as decoration, carved or in relief. They may be found, for example, around the outside of font bowls where they provide settings for a series of figure sculptures in the sections beneath.

Arch
Curved or pointed construction of wedge-shaped stones or bricks. It may divide tower, aisles, transepts, chapels, chancel, etc, from the nave of the church. The stones are supported by mutual pressure and, in turn, can sustain a weight of masonry from above over an opening. Early arches are round-headed, and the structures become more pointed as the architecture develops.

Arch brace

Arch brace
The curved member between the collar beam and the wall post in a roof. The term is often loosely used to describe any piece of timber which supports another.

Architectural styles
General development of design and construction within certain periods. See under Decorated; Early English; Elizabethan; Greek Revival; Hanoverian; Jacobean; Neo-Gothic; Norman; Perpendicular; Renaissance; Saxon; Transitional; Tudor; Twentieth-century; Victorian.

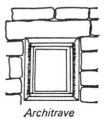

Architrave

ARCH SHAPES

Simple primitive, two-stone abutment

two-stone type with keystones

stilted

three-centred

double primitive, several abutments

early round with single lintel

round

four-centred

flat type, single lintel

double round, wedge-shaped stones

rollock

cusped

flat type, single lintel, wedge-shaped

segment

blunt

horseshoe

flat type of wedge-shaped stones

bell-shaped

equilateral

pointed horseshoe

flat type of wedge-shaped and squared stones

semi-circular

lancet

ogee

ARCH SHAPES

8

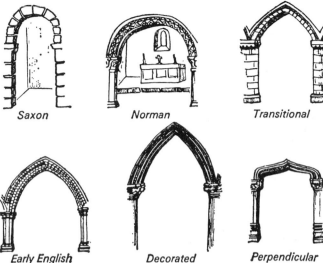

Saxon *Norman* *Transitional*

Early English *Decorated* *Perpendicular*

ARCH TYPES

Architrave
Main beam resting on the uppermost member of a capital or the moulding around arches, doorways or windows.

Archivolt
Decorative moulding which follows the contour of an arch face impost to impost.

Arch ordering
Set of overlapping, concentric steps in the shape of an arch.

Arcosolia
Burial chamber

Arcuated
Curved in the shape of a bow.

Armature
Medieval iron framework which supports the stained glass in windows which have no stone tracery.

Arris
The sharp edge which is formed at the point where two wedge-shaped or curved pieces of stone or wood meet.

Perpendicular

Archivolt

9

Art Nouveau
Extravagant and floral decoration of the late Victorian and Edwardian years. This was often used in overwhelming profusion in church carving, panels, reredoses, etc, which were made around 1900.

Ashlar
Varying sizes of squared stone blocks, sawn or hewn to a smooth face and joined together. The blocks usually have a large face area, even if they are not very thick. They are skilfully put together in level courses and used to surface exterior walls of coarser masonry.

Ashlar

Ashlar piece
Short upright supporting post between the inner wall plate and a rafter in a wooden roof.

Atlantes
Sculptured figure of a man used as a pillar.

Atrium
Covered colonnade before the door of a church.

Bale tomb

Auditory plan
A style of church-building which allowed everyone taking part in the service to be accommodated in one undivided interior. It was a feature of the Classical seventeenth century.

Aumbry
Small cupboard, set of cupboards or recess built into the south or east wall of the church, but usually near the altar. They hold the ornaments or sacred vessels which are used at mass or communion.

Ball flower

Axial tower
Central tower which is built above the choir.

Baldachino
Canopy above an altar and projecting over it. May be suspended from the ceiling or supported by columns.

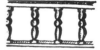

Balustrade

Bale tomb
Table tomb surmounted by an incised roll top, at each end of which is a scallop inset by a skull.

Ball flower
Type of ornamentation which resembles a small ball, half enclosed by a globular flower which has three incurved petals. The whole is used at regular intervals in concave moulding and was a feature of the Decorated period.

Barge and barge board

Baluster
Small vertical column or stone strip — usually fatter in the middle or at the base. One of a series used to support a rail.

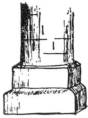

Balustrade
Whole series of small vertical columns or stone strips which support a handrail.

Banner cupboard
Also known as banner stave locker. Large cupboard or wall recess which was used in medieval times to store banners and processional crosses.

Norman

Baptistery see Baptistry

Baptistry
Section of the church — usually at the west end — which is reserved for the administration of the sacrament of baptism and contains the font.

Barge
Overhanging exterior section of a roof which projects from, and runs the whole length of, the slope of a gable.

13th century

Barge board
Ornamental piece of timber on the gable of a wooden porch or roof, where the covering of the roof extends over the wall. It is so positioned to hide any exposed ends of horizontal roof beams.

Baroque
Style of European architecture which developed a greater freedom and exuberance in its design than during the earlier Renaissance. It originated in late sixteenth-century Italy and Spain and continued until the first half of the eighteenth century.

14th century

Barrel vault
Semicircular or curved chamber or roof with dual parallel lateral thrust and the same outline from all angles.

Bar tracery
The simple pattern formed by continuing upwards the vertical members which divide a window into its lights. One of the earliest forms of ornamental stonework, which superseded plate tracery in the middle of the thirteenth century.

Base
Lowest section of a pier or column, between the shaft

15th century

BASE

and the ground. It comprises the plinth and associated moulding.

Basilica
Properly a two-celled church which is built on a double colonnade and apse plan. The term is also used to describe any building which is used as a Christian church.

Bas-relief
The effect achieved by a slightly raised sculpture.

Batter
Slight but regular inward slope of a wall from the base upwards.

*Base
(Renaissance)*

Battlements
Indented wall above a tower or the roof of a nave, consisting of alternate and equal solid and open areas. See also Embrasure and Merlon.

Bay
Section of an arcade between two consecutive pillars, columns, pilasters or beams.

Beak head
Form of decoration depicting the head of a bird or animal with a long beak which extends over a convex moulding. Typical Norman work and repeated at regular intervals.

Bay

Bed head see Grave board

Belfry
Part of the church tower, turret, or a detached building which contains the church bells.

Belfry louvre see Louvre

Beak head

Bell
Hollow structure of cast metal which contains a clapper. This causes a musical note as it strikes against the inside of the bell when it is rung.

Bell capital
Headstone of a column so moulded that the result resembles the appearance of an upturned bell.

Bellcote
Small tower or arch which contains bells. Generally such are to be found at the west end of the church, or at the east end of the nave roof in the case of a sanctus bell.

Bell capital

Bench
Long, plain, flat seating of wood or stone. There is often a similar backrest running the length of the seat, or else it is built against a wall.

Bench-end
Vertical part of the bench which is adjacent to an aisle. Most of them are square-headed and they are often richly or quaintly carved, depicting people, events, biblical scenes and even mythical characters. The best are in Cornwall.

Bequest board
A notice — usually painted on wood — which describes some fund or local charity. May be found anywhere in the church but commonly affixed to the interior wall of the tower.

Bible box
Locked box in which the great church bible could be kept for protection. Invariably richly carved.

Billet
Norman moulding consisting of short, raised rectangles repeated at regular intervals.

Blind arcade
Row of unpierced arches attached to a wall in order to strengthen or decorate it. Those intended for decoration are often richly carved.

Blind clerestory
Structure formed by extending the wall of the nave above the roof of the aisle without adding windows along its length.

Blind storey see Blind triforium

Blind tracery
Lines drawn out on solid, unperforated masonry.

Blind triforium
Area of blank, unpierced wall surface above a nave arcade but below the clerestory.

Block capital
Cube-shaped head to a Romanesque column or pilaster. The lower angles are rounded to meet the circular supporting shaft below.

Boarded chest
Rough, rectangular box formed by affixing large planks to timber end-pieces with wrought iron nails.

Bellcote

Bench-end

Billet

Blind arcade

Blind triforium

13

BOARDED CHEST

This was a thirteenth-century improvement on the monoxylon.

Bonding
Binding masonry which structurally effects a union of walls.

Bone hole see Charnel house

Boss
Projecting ornament which is placed at the intersection of ribs in a vault or roof in order to disguise the point at which they join. Bosses are usually carved with foliage or figures, made in wood or stone, and painted.

Bosses

Bowtells
Rounded edges to the receding mouldings in an arch, etc (see also Arch ordering).

Box pew
Bench seat set in a high, plain, wooden enclosure most often with a door.

Brace
Slanting or curved timber used to support, strengthen or bring together the main roof timbers.

Bracket
Flat-topped projection at right angles to the surface of a wall, used to support some horizontal member from underneath.

Box pews

Brass
Sepulchral memorial made by cutting the likeness of a dead person on the surface of a brass sheet, inlaid in a stone slab. Usually on the floor or wall of the church to mark the spot where the person is interred. The oldest — dated 1277 — is at Stoke D'Abernon, Surrey.

Brattishing
Carved openwork in a parapet or on the solid part of battlements.

Bressumer beam

Bressumer beam
Low beam which extends horizontally across the front of a gallery or over an opening. It supports the frame of a floor above.

Broach
Elongated half pyramid of masonry between the

Cable mouldings

14

corner angle of an unparapeted tower and one side of the octagonal spire above.

Broach spire
Octagonal spire rising from the top of a tower without a parapet. The triangular space at each angle is covered by masonry inclined from each right angle on the base to a point along each diagonal side of the octagon.

Broach spire

Bullnose moulding
Rounded or blunt moulding which has no particular shape.

Buttress
Stone or brick support which gives additional strength to a wall and counteracts its outward thrust.

Cable moulding
Decoration which takes the form of a twisted cord. It sometimes looks like loosely intertwined string but is more often thick and rolled.

Caen stone
Fine-grained limestone which came from Normandy and was used in English medieval church-building.

Campanile

Camber
Horizontal beam which has a slight upwards curve in order to prevent the structure it supports from sagging.

Came
Grooved strip of lead indented to accommodate the small pieces of glass used in lattice windows.

Campanile
Detached or isolated bell-tower.

Canopy

Candelabra
Holder for candles in several arms radiating from a central stem.

Canopy
Covering above an altar, tomb, pulpit, niche, etc; ornamental and sometimes highly decorated.

Canopy of honour see Ceilure

Capital
Large carved headstone of a column or pilaster which supports arches or vaulting ribs. Often richly carved with foliated, human or animal designs.

Candelabra

Cardinal
North, south, east and west. The points of the compass as usually applied to appendages on a particular feature.

Carrel
Open or closed closet or pew in the bay of a cloister used for study or meditation.

Cartouche
Marble wall tablet in the shape of a scroll. It usually contains an inscription and is sometimes elaborately framed.

Norman

Caryatid
Figure of a woman used as a pillar.

Castellated
Adorned with a series of battlements.

Cathedral
Principal or mother church of a diocese which is the seat of a bishop.

Transitional

Cavetto
Concave moulding.

Ceilure
Part of a wagon roof above an altar or rood which is decoratively panelled to draw attention to the feature beneath.

Celtic plan
Simple single or two-celled plan of church building with characteristically high walls in relation to the ground area.

Early English

Censer
Vessel in which incense is burnt.

Centring
Temporary wooden framework which is used to support an arch, vault or dome whilst it is being constructed.

14th century

Chalice
Wine goblet used in the celebration of holy communion.

Chamfer
The result of cutting away to any width the sharp edge which is formed where two blocks of wood or stone meet at right angles.

15th century

Chancel
Eastern continuation of the nave which usually contains the altar and is reserved for the clergy and the choir. The name is derived from the cancelli or screens which separated it from the rest of the building, and many are still railed off or gained by mounting steps.

Cartouche

Chancel arch
Single span at the west end of the chancel, dividing it from the nave.

Chancel screen
Partition from floor level which divides the chancel from the nave. Such screens are usually highly decorated (especially in Devonshire), have doors and are made of wood or stone.

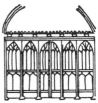

Chalice.

Chandelier
Arrangement or cluster of artificial lights, radiating from a central source and suspended from the roof.

Chantry chapel
Small chapel or side altar in which masses are said for the soul of the person who endowed it. Such areas often include the tomb of the donor and may be found in a separate building or as part of the aisle of the church.

Chapter house
Polygonal or rectangular room in a cathedral, used by the dean and canons to conduct their business transactions.

Chancel screen

Charnel house
Crypt, vault or cellar in which are piled bones removed from the churchyard.

Chest
Large box, usually of oak and often well carved, in which the church kept the parish documents, valuables and subscriptions. Many contain ancient padlocks; at one time every church had at least one.

Chest

Chevet
French word for an apse; used to describe a semicircular or polygonal east end with chapels radiating from it.

Chevron
Zigzag pattern characteristic of Norman decorative moulding.

Chevron

Choir
Section of the church occupied by the choristers and the clergy. This is usually the eastern arm of the building, and for this reason a section of the chancel is sometimes called the choir even when it is not strictly used for that purpose.

Chrismatory
Receptacle for the consecrated oils.

Christ's board
Early name for the wooden tables which preceded stone altars.

Churchyard cross

Church registers see Parish registers

Churchyard
Enclosure surrounding the church and sometimes used for burials. Circular ones often indicate that the area is an ancient, pre-Christian burial ground.

Churchyard cross
Stone cross which was erected to the south of all pre-Reformation churches to denote consecrated ground. Some were very tall and beautifully carved, although only the shaft now remains of most. Cornwall is particularly rich in this feature.

Ciborium

Ciborium
Canopy built above, or as part of a shrine. The term is also used to describe a similarly shaped covered container which is used for the consecrated elements in the Eucharist.

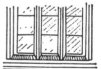

Cill

Cill
Horizontal base member of a window or screen.

Cinquefoil
Five-cusped ornamental filling for a circle or arch.

Cinquefoil

Clamp buttress
Shallow flat-sided wall brace which is more decorative than supporting. It is usually to be found at the corners of the building.

Clasping buttress
Supporting structure which entirely encloses — equally on both sides — the right angle formed where two walls meet.

Classical architecture
Style and decoration in the manner of Greek and Roman architecture, as opposed to Gothic influence.

Clamp buttress

Classicism see Classical architecture
Clear storey see Clerestory

Clerestory
Structure formed by continuing the walls of the nave
above and away from the roof of an adjoining aisle,
and adding windows with the purpose of letting more
light into the church.

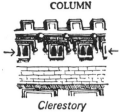
COLUMN

Clerestory

Clock jack
Mechanical figure which chimes the time on bells by
striking them with a hammer or one of its feet.

Cloister
Covered walk or arcade which usually runs around
the sides of a quadrangle and is often vaulted.

Cob
Mixture of clay and straw used for building walls.

Coffer
Decorated, sunken ceiling panel.

Coffin
Oblong container in which a corpse is buried.

Coffin table
Raised oblong of stone under the lychgate or at the
entrance to the churchyard, used to rest the coffin.

Clock jack

Collar beam
Horizontal timber which connects a pair of principal
rafters just below their highest point.

Collecting box
Small wooden box for the collection of various
offerings; these days used for the fabric fund, and
the price of books, pamphlets and parish magazines.
Usually sited just inside the main doorway, unless the
church is a very large one. Older collecting boxes are
sometimes protected by wrought iron.

Collegiate church
Church endowed for canons or as a cathedral church,
but without a see. Served in the Middle Ages by a
staff of clergy.

Coffin table

Colonnade
Row of columns.

Column
Cylindrical, vertical pillar which usually supports an
arch.

Collar beam

Common rafter
Sloping beam in a roof, which connects the horizontal ridge piece to the sole plate at the top of a supporting wall.

Communion table
Wooden table which was used in the place of an altar in Elizabethan and Jacobean times. Often nicely decorated, and situated in the middle of the chancel.

Common rafters

Composite see Order

Compound pier
Independent group of columns and angles of masonry.

Conoid
Cone-shaped section of fan vaulting.

Consecration cross
One of twelve usually incised or painted on the interior and exterior walls of the church at its dedication.

Coping
Uppermost, covered course of an exterior wall. Sometimes flat, but more usually sloping to discharge rain, etc.

Compound pier

Corbel
Short block of stone or timber which projects from a wall in order to support a beam, an arch or any horizontal feature. Often carved or moulded.

Corbel table
Row of exterior or interior corbels supporting a roof, parapet or cornice — and usually connected. Corbel tables are a feature of Norman work.

Corbel

Corbie steps see Crow steps

Corinthian see Order

Cornice
Highest horizontal moulding on a wall, or above a column.

Corbel table

Corona
Circular band of metal or wood which contains candles around the rim and is usually hung from the roof. This is also a general architectural term for the projecting part of the highest horizontal wall moulding or cornice.

Cornice

Corpse gate see Lychgate

Cove
Concave arch, or the junction of a ceiling and wall.

Cover paten
Receptacle for the consecrated bread of communion, made from the cover of a communion cup.

Coving
Usually the curved junction of a ceiling and wall, but also used to describe the under surface of an arch.

Cradle roof see Wagon roof

Cradle vault see Barrel vault

Credence
Small shelf or table used to hold sacred items. Such shelves are usually to be found built into the wall near the altar, and often as part of a thirteenth-century piscina.

Crenellation
The appearance of a series of battlements.

Cresset stone
Stone slabs in which several hollows (cressets) have been scooped out to accommodate burning wicks floating on fat.

Crest or **Cresting**
Ornamental horizontal band along the top of a screen.

Crocket
Projecting buds, flowers, curled leaves or bunches of foliage usually carved and placed at regular intervals along the sloping sides of arches, canopies, spires, finials, pinnacles, gables, etc. Decoration to break up a flat skyline, but which also served a useful purpose in affording some foothold for masons.

Crocket capital
Early English column which was decorated by single buds, flowers or curled leaves at regular intervals.

Cross
Emblem of the Christian church which is always the centre piece of any altar and is to be found carved, painted and in relief at almost any other point within the church and its environs.

Coving

Credence shelf

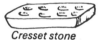

Cresset stone

Crest

Crockets

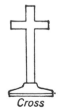

Cross

Crossing
Area formed by the intersection of transepts, chancel and nave.

Cross vault
Structure formed where two barrel vaults meet at right angles.

Cross window
Window divided into four sections by only one horizontal bar, and one vertical bar.

Cross window

Crow steps
Steps in a battlement or gable.

Cruciform
Church plan in the shape of a cross, with a central tower between the transept arms.

Crypt
Chamber or vault, usually beneath the east end of the church and sometimes containing an altar.

Crow steps

Cupola
Dome-shaped roof or polygonal turret.

Cushion cap
Early Norman type of capital with a square upper section but rounded into an ornamented convex shape towards the pillar below.

Crypt

Cusp
Small projecting point at the intersection of arcs in the tracery of Gothic windows and arches.

Cylindrical vault see Barrel vault

Dado
Loosely used to describe any decoration on the lower section of a wall surface.

Cupola

Dagger decoration
Fourteenth-century tracery which takes the form of a spearhead, cusped and arched on the inside.

Daub
Coating of mud and clay. See also Wattle and daub.

Deambulatory see Ambulatory

Decalogue
Fixture containing the ten commandments, Lord's prayer or creed.

Cushion cap

Decorated period
About 1272 to 1350. Second period of English Gothic church architecture noted for heightening and widening existing aisles, the addition of parapets, pinnacles and porches. Window tracery became ornate and divided by mullions. Arcade pillars were more slender, vaulting more complex and pinnacles and crockets appeared. Exeter Cathedral is a good example of building in this period.

Cusp

Dedication
The name of a saint or especial event which is given to each church for convenience.

Demi-angel
Relief depicting the upper part of an angel appearing out of the clouds.

Demi-column
Half of a shaft which projects from a flat wall.

Detached tower
Tower which is built — usually in order to overcome some difficulties in geographical location — away from the rest of the church.

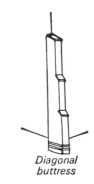
Diagonal buttress

Devil's door
Small entrance in the north wall of the church. Although most of them are now bricked up, they were once left open at baptism to allow the child's evil spirits to leave. Also used for processions at the same service, and at funerals.

Diagonal buttress
Projecting exterior support at the point where two walls meet, but not enclosing the angle formed at that point.

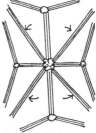
Diagonal ribs

Diagonal ribs
Arched members which run at right angles from corner to corner across the bay of a vault.

Diamond ornament
Norman decoration, in the form of a continuous band of diamond shapes.

Diamond ornament

Diamond pane
Small pieces of glass which, when inserted into a lead frame prepared to receive them, form a lattice window.

Diaper
Orderly, repetitive and comprehensive decoration of

Diaper

squares or diamonds, carved in low relief or painted on a plain wall surface.

Dog tooth

Dissolution
Term applied to Henry VIII's two-part suppression of the monasteries, and appropriation of their lands.

Dole cupboard

Dog tooth
Late Norman and Early English repetitive decoration around doorways and arches. It takes the form of groups of two or four tooth-like ornaments in a hollow moulding, set diagonally to each other and repeated continuously or at short intervals.

Dole cupboard
Cupboard which originated in medieval times to store bread for travellers and the poor of the parish.

Domical vault
Arched roof or ceiling shaped like a dome.

Dormer window

Doom painting
Frightening portrayal of the Day of Judgement. A feature of churches in the Middle Ages, as was interior painting generally. Those extant, and in some cases only fragments which remain, are usually to be found on the chancel arch.

Doric see Order

Double hammerbeam roof

Dormer
An upright window which projects from a sloping roof.

Double-framed roof
One in which the rafters, etc, which comprise the cross section, are joined along its length by other members.

Double ogee moulding

Double hammerbeam roof
Structure in which there are two stages of roof braces which rest on right-angled, hammer-shaped supports.

Double ogee
Design formed by a double moulding, concave and convex, round and shallow.

Double splay window
Window placed centrally in a thick wall so that the masonry slopes away from it towards both the interior and the exterior wall surfaces.

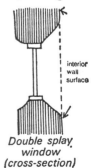

Double splay window (cross-section)

24

Double tracery
One layer of ornamental stonework between windows, etc, superimposed upon another.

Dowel
Headless oak or metal pin used to secure wood or stone members together.

Dripstone

Dripstone
Ornamental stone moulding above a doorway, arch or window to throw off the rainwater and prevent it from running down the walls. See also Hood moulding and Label stop.

Drum
General term for a vertical interior wall which encloses a circular or polygonal area. Often applied to the similar part of a dome or dome-shaped roof.

Drum

Early English period
About 1170 to 1300. First period of English Gothic church architecture, noted for the appearance of the pointed arch and lancet windows. These were constructed in groups of three, five or seven, and were without mullions. At the same time the cruciform plan became common in larger churches and elsewhere chancels were lengthened. Mouldings were deeply cut and clusters of pillars around a central core typified the era. Delicately carved foliage and dog-tooth ornamentation were popular. Salisbury Cathedral is an example of building in this period.

East end

East end
Wall of the church against which the altar is usually placed.

Easter sepulchre
Tomb or recess used to house the consecrated host from Good Friday to Easter morning. Often beautifully adorned.

Easter sepulchre

East window
Usually the largest window in the church, and to be found behind the main altar. Many contain magnificent medieval stained glass.

Eaves

Eaves
Underside of a sloping roof where it overhangs the wall below.

Effigy
Any sculptured likeness of a person, created in stone, brass, marble, alabaster, etc.

Effigy

25

Eighteenth-century see Greek Revival, Hanoverian

Eighth-century see Saxon

Eleventh-century see Saxon, Norman

Embattled moulding

Elizabethan period
About 1560 to 1600. Really a part of Renaissance and not usually applied to church architecture in the same sense. However, some notable woodwork, especially panelling, was done during this time.

Embattled moulding
Ornamental moulding of the Norman period, depicting a raised outline resembling battlements.

Embrasure
Opening in the battlements of a parapet. The word is normally used in connection with fortifications but church battlements were used as lookout posts.

Encaustic tiles
Glazed clay tiles of varying colours used on the floor of the church.

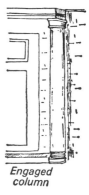

Engaged column

Engaged column
Vertical pillar or shaft which is partly let into a wall.

Engaged shaft as Engaged column

English Gothic see Gothic

Entablature
Order above a column which includes the horizontal mouldings such as cornice and frieze, also the architrave.

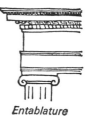

Entablature

Entasis
Slight convex curve given to the shaft of a column in order to correct the visual illusion that straight lines are concave.

Epitaph
Comment to be found on tombstones and wall plaques. Usually takes the form of a strange or humorous rhyme which describes the character or the fate of the deceased.

Escutcheon see Funeral hatchment

Extrados
Outside or highest curve of an arch, opposite the soffit.

Epitaph

Facade
Exterior surface of a building; usually applied to the main side of the building which faces a street.

Family pew
Fine arrangement of seats in the church which were set aside for the use of a local family. These are especially plush and well upholstered in churches adjacent to country houses which were once the seats of the lords of the manor.

Fan vaulting

Fan vaulting
Ultimate development in English Gothic vaulting, confined to the Perpendicular period. Decoration takes the form of trumpet-shaped, inverted semi-cones of masonry in fan-like shapes, enriched by tracery and springing equally in all directions.

Feather edge
Finely tapered edge of a wedge-shaped board which is inserted into the V-shaped opening of an adjacent plank.

Feathering
Row of small arcs which are separated at each intersection by projecting points and applied as the decoration on an arch.

Feathering

Fenestration
Arrangement of windows.

Feretory
Tomb or coffin for the remains of a saint. Sometimes the chapel or an area behind the main altar in which such a receptacle is placed.

Fillet

Fifteenth-century see Gothic, Perpendicular, Tudor, Renaissance.

Fillet
Small flat moulding which either horizontally or vertically divides two others. May also be cut on the surface of a larger moulding or around a pier.

Finial

Finial
Usually leaf-like decoration which forms the terminal at the top of a gable, canopy, bench-end, tower corner, etc. Originated in the fourteenth century.

Flagon
Large vessel used to hold the wine at the celebration of the Eucharist.

Flagon

FLIER

Flier see Flying buttress

Flowing tracery
Ornamental stonework of the late Decorated period; the form did not include circular or ogee shapes.

Flushwork
Carved or cut stone or flint used as surface ornamentation.

Fluted
Bevelled or grooved.

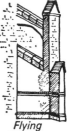

Flying buttress
Open half-arch or arch which either bridges two walls or connects a wall across the roof of an aisle to the main buttress.

Flying buttress

Foil
Area between the projecting points in a traceried ornament. See also Cinquefoil, Quatrefoil, Trefoil.

Foil

Foliated
Carved with a leafy ornamentation. Mostly applied to crockets, finials and capitals.

Font
Structure designed to hold the holy water which is used at the sacrament of baptism. Most are made of stone, but a few lead ones survive and even less of copper and bronze.

Foliated

Font canopy
Wooden screen which completely surrounds a font.

Font cover
Protective cover for the font when it is not in use. Most are simple, flat constructions, carved in wood. There are many beautifully carved examples which tower into the air.

Footstone
Small incised stone at the opposite end of the grave to the headstone. Usually contains brief details of the deceased such as the initials and the date of death.

Font cover

Foundations
Stones or concrete below ground level which are used to support the weight of the building above.

Four-centred arch
Head of a doorway, window, etc, which springs from four points.

Four-centred arch

Four-leafed flower

Decoration consisting of a small ball in the centre of four equal, joining leaves. Ornamentation characteristic of the Decorated period.

Four-leafed flower

Fourteenth-century see Early English, Decorated, Gothic, Perpendicular.

pre-Conquest	*pre-Conquest*	*pre-Conquest*	*Norman*
Norman	*Norman*	*Norman*	*Norman*
Norman	*Early English*	*Early English*	*Decorated*
Decorated	*Perpendicular*	*post-Reformation*	*post-Reformation*

FONTS

Freestone
Extremely finely grained stone which can be broken or cut in any direction.

Fresco
Wall painting which was executed before the plaster underneath had properly dried out. Also loosely applied to any wall painting.

Frieze

Frieze
Carved band of ornamentation worked horizontally on a wall surface immediately below the cornice.

Frontal see Altar frontal

Funeral hatchment
Diamond-shaped painting — usually on board — which depicts the arms or family crest of the deceased against a background which shows both the sex and marital status of the person involved.

Funeral hatchment

Gable
Any triangular-shaped canopy over doors, windows, sedilia, piscina, etc, but almost always applied to the triangular upper section of the exterior wall at the end of a building.

Gable

Gable cross
Stone cross placed above a gable.

Galilee
Small porch or chapel built at the entrance or west end of a church.

Gallery
Covered upper storey above an aisle or at the west end of the nave. After the Reformation this area was often used by the village orchestra.

Galilee

Gargoyle
Sometimes seen as Gurgoyle. Carved stone waterspouts, built outwards from the gutter or side of the church in order to throw water clear from the roof. Some support a rainwater pipe; most are carved in the form of animals, grotesques or mythical beasts, although some less ambitious examples do portray human heads.

Garth
Open space surrounded by cloisters.

Geometrical tracery
The bar and plate tracery of the Early English

Gallery

period, which filled the upper parts of the windows with their own particular forms. These simple beginnings soon gave way to many and various shapes.

Gnomon
Rod at the centre of a mass dial. The time of day is indicated by the position of its shadow as the sun falls across the rod.

God's acre
A churchyard.

God's board see Christ's board

Gothic
The long period of architecture which exists from the twelfth to the fifteenth centuries and embodied the Early English and Decorated styles. The original influence was the architecture of twelfth-century France.

Gothic Revival
Serious attempts by early nineteenth-century designers to build in the true Gothic style.

Graffiti
Varied and ancient drawings, markings, etc, to be found on windows, doorways, buttresses.

Grain
Texture and arrangement of fibres in a piece of stone or wood.

Grate see Grille

Grave
Recess or hole in the ground containing a corpse or corpses for which it was prepared, filled in and usually with a slight mound above ground level.

Grave board
Narrow piece of wood supported by stilts at each end, and used in the place of a headstone to record biographical details of the deceased.

Gravestone
Variously shaped stone marking the place of a grave.

Greek Revival
Period of church and domestic building along Classical lines which flourished in England from c 1760 to 1820.

Gargoyle

Geometrical tracery

Gnomon

Grave board

Gravestones

31

Grid tracery
The effect of narrow upright windows or openings with cusped heads set in tracery and usually divided by a horizontal member.

Grille

Grille
Wrought iron or similarly decorated screen, often with gates or doors, and used to protect a tomb.

Grisaille
Type of stained-glass window painting, using greyish-white glass and monochrome decoration fired into the glass in a neutral-coloured enamel.

Groined vault

Groin
Plain edge formed by two intersecting vaults.

Groined vault
Structure resulting from the right-angled intersection of two tunnel vaults.

Gurgoyle see Gargoyle

Hagioscope

Hagioscope
Hole made in a wall or pillar between an aisle and the chancel so that the main altar can be seen through it. Also known as a squint.

Hall church
Building in which the main body of the church and the aisles are of about equal height.

Hammerbeam roof

Hammerbeam
Projecting, right-angled, hammer-shaped beam or bracket at the foot of the curved member and principal rafter in a wooden roof. Some are decorated, and they often support vertical or arched braces.

Hanoverian period
Not a style applied generally to parish-church architecture but may be taken as building between 1689 and 1760.

Haunch

Hatchment see Funeral hatchment

Haunch
Part of an arch between the pillar from which it springs and the highest or central point.

Headstone

Headstone
Variously shaped stone at the head of an exterior grave. Usually takes the form of a memorial and

includes biographical details of the departed, often together with an epitaph.

Herringbone

Herringbone
Pattern formed on masonry by a zigzag of diagonally placed stones alternately inclining to the left and right.

Herse
Metal framework over a coffin or tomb, containing holes for candles. These were lighted and prayers were said at the anniversary of the deceased.

Hipped roof

High altar
Principal altar of a church in which there are more than one.

Hipped roof
Roof structure of sloping instead of vertical sides and ends.

Hood moulding

Hog's back
Type of carved Saxon gravestone.

Holy water stoop see Stoup

Hood moulding
Gothic ornamental stone moulding which projects over an arch, doorway, window, etc, in order to throw water clear of the building.

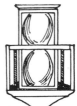
Hour glass

Hour glass
Waisted glass of sand, usually to be found by the side of the pulpit and attached to it by an ornamental iron bracket. Introduced later in the sixteenth century in order to time sermons.

Impost
Moulded upper member of a pillar which carries an arch; the point from which an arch springs.

Impost

Indent
Any shallow area which has been chiselled out of a flat surface but usually to allow a brass to be placed flush with the surrounding stonework.

Intersecting tracery
The shape formed — in Early English windows — where several mullions in the same window branch into Y shapes, and continue with equal curves. The effect is that each group of two or more lancet windows which result forms a pointed arch.

Intersecting tracery

3

Intrados see Soffit

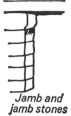

Ionic see Order

Jacobean period
Renaissance influence during the reign of James I (1603-25). This included extensive use of classic orders and features and is noted mainly for attractively carved woodwork, screens, and especially canopied pulpits, of which many survive.

Jamb and jamb stones

Jamb
Straight upright side-post of a doorway, or the side of an arch window.

Jamb stones
Masonry blocks forming the side of a doorway, etc.

Jesse window
Representation of the genealogy of Christ in either stonework or stained glass.

Jube
Rood screen which includes a pulpit as part of its structure.

Keystone

Kentish tracery
Ornamental stonework in a particular star-like form, with very elaborate cusping.

Kerb
Stone edging to mark the boundary of a grave.

King post

Keystone
Centre stone at the crossing of the ribs of a vault or a round arch. Often decorated.

King post
Vertical beam in a wooden roof which connects the tie beam to the junction of the rafters above.

Label and label stop

Kneeler
That section of the moulding around the face of an arch which continues horizontally along the member or impost from which the arch springs.

Label
Ornamental stone moulding over a Perpendicular square-headed window.

Label stop
Decoratively carved end to the dripstone or hood moulding.

Lancet windows

Lady chapel
Chapel dedicated to the Virgin, usually to the east of the main altar in a large church.

Lancet window
Tall, narrow light which is sharply pointed at the top and a feature of Early English architecture. Often to be found in groups of three and five; groups of seven are less common.

Lantern cross
Churchyard cross, usually with a several-sided lantern shape at the top. The lantern itself usually contained sculptures or decorations in each of its sides and was surmounted by some other decoration.

Lantern cross

Lantern tower
Tower which is extended vertically with a lighthouse-like structure, illuminated by upper windows.

Lattice window
Window constructed of diamond-shaped panes set in diagonal lead strips. See also Came, Diamond pane.

Lattice window

Laudian rails
Railings which were placed around wooden altar tables in the seventeenth century by order of Archbishop William Laud.

Lean-to roof
Roof with only one slope, adjoining a higher wall.

Lectern
Reading stand to support the church bible. May take the form of a desk, but is commonly designed as an eagle with outstretched wings.

Lean-to roof

Ledger stone
Large flat slab over a grave and sometimes let into the floor of the church. Often includes a coat of arms and an interesting inscription.

Lent veil
Curtain which was hung across the sanctuary during Lent.

Lepers' window
Low side window on the south side of the chancel. It was so named from the belief that lepers, who could not enter the church, used it to see the mass in progress. The position of most such windows proves this to be untrue.

Lectern

Lierne rib
Short vaulting rib which crosses from one boss to another and — with others — effects a star-like shape. Particular decorative characteristic of the late fourteenth century.

Lierne vault
Vault decorated by lierne ribs.

Lierne ribs

Light
Wall opening for the purpose of letting in light; a window or the spaces created by dividing a window with vertical bars known as mullions.

Linenfold panelling
Series of wooden panels, carved to look like pieces of material hanging vertically in their natural folds.

Lintel
Flat horizontal stone or beam which spans a window opening or the top of a door.

Lithic
Of, or pertaining to stone.

Linenfold panels

Long and short work
Large vertical stone slabs which alternate with horizontal ones to form the angle where two walls meet in Saxon work.

Longitudinal strut
Vertical timber between the main beam and the ridge piece in a timber roof.

Lintel

Louvre
Horizontal sloping boards which allow air but no light into belfry windows.

Low side window
Unglazed opening in the south wall of the chancel, built to assist ventilation.

Lintel

Lozenge moulding
Ornamental moulding of diamond shapes, joining each other in a continuous line. A feature of Norman decoration.

Lucarne see Spire light

Lychgate
Covered entrance to the churchyard. Originally provided shelter for the shrouded bodies, and later a resting place for the coffin to await the priest.

Long and short work

tie beam

Longitudinal
strut

Mason
Craftsman who works in stone.

Mason's mark
Trade mark or 'signature' of a mason or his descendants.

Mason stop
Right-angled end-piece on the ornamental stone moulding above a doorway or window.

Mass dial
Sundial which told the time by the position of the shadow from a central rod, on lines radiating in the stonework from its base. The hour for mass is usually marked by a deeper groove.

Louvred
windows

Medallion
Large circular or oval-shaped medal, panel or tablet. Used to depict a biblical scene, symbol, figure of a saint, etc.

Medallion moulding
Pictorial, medal-shaped, ornamental moulding of the Norman period.

Lychgate

Mensa
Stone altar slab, sometimes marked with consecration crosses.

Mercy seat see Misericord

Merlon
Raised section in the battlements of a parapet. Such may be solid, pierced, panelled or carved. They are spaced at regular intervals and were used for shelter.

Mason stop

Minster
Large church which was originally attached to a monastery.

Minstrel gallery see Musician's gallery

Medallion moulding

Misericord or **Miserere**
Carved bracket which supports a hinged seat when it is turned up for use. Often beautifully ornamented with both ecclesiastical subjects and the more grotesque and eccentric. A feature of choir stalls. Hereford Cathedral has the most famous examples.

Merlon

Monoxylon
Dug-out chest, roughly carved from the trunk of a tree. Saxon and Norman work.

Misericord

Monstrance
Open vessel in which the sacred host is shown.

Monument
Generally any permanent item which commemorates a person or event. More usually used to describe an effigy or carving which depicts the likenesses of people.

Mortesafe
Stone or iron vault which was erected around a churchyard tomb to prevent the body inside from being carried off by body snatchers.

Mortise
Hole cut into a piece of timber to receive exactly the end or tenon of an adjoining piece, so carved to fit into it.

Mouchette
Fourteenth-century tracery basically in the shape of a curved spearhead, cusped and arched on the inside.

Moulding
Contoured outline which adds beauty and tone — through light and shade contrasts — to projections, cornices, pillars, windows, arches, etc.

Mounting steps
Steps placed at the entrance to the church path in order that visitors could dismount more easily from their horses.

Mullion
Slender vertical bar which divides a window into two or more lights.

Multifoil
Arrangement of several cusped ornamental fillings for a circle or arch.

Muntin
Vertical member in a wooden screen which either supports the head beam or frames the panelling.

Mural painting
Colourful wall decoration which depicts religious events, etc.

Musician's gallery
Upper storey above an aisle or at the west end of the nave. The area was used by small village bands during the seventeenth, eighteenth and early nineteenth centuries.

Monument

Mouchette

Mullion stone pillar dividing Norman windows

Mullion dividing a 13th-century window

Multifoil

Nail head
Ornamental moulding of the late Norman period, consisting of raised pyramidal shapes in a continuous sequence.

Nail head

Narthex
Enclosed, sacred, single-storey vestibule at the western end of the church. Sometimes a covered porch at the main entrance, which was used only by women in early churches.

Nave
Main body or the western arm of the church in which the congregation is housed during services. Comprises the area between the chancel and the west end.

Nave

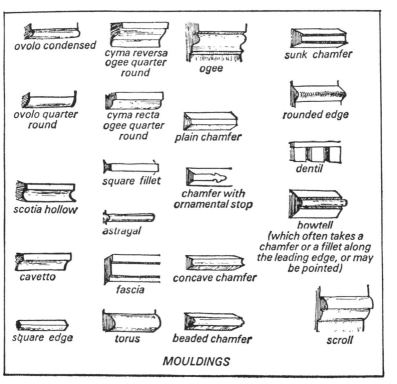

ovolo condensed

cyma reversa ogee quarter round

ogee

sunk chamfer

ovolo quarter round

cyma recta ogee quarter round

plain chamfer

rounded edge

square fillet

chamfer with ornamental stop

dentil

scotia hollow

astragal

bowtell
(which often takes a chamfer or a fillet along the leading edge, or may be pointed)

cavetto

fascia

concave chamfer

square edge

torus

beaded chamfer

scroll

MOULDINGS

Needle spire
Particularly narrow conical structure which is built from the tower roof but well within any parapet.

Neo-Gothic period
Late eighteenth-century style of church-building which had a frivolous approach in both design and materials to the true Gothic.

Needle spire

Neo-Greek Revival
Late eighteenth-century church-building in the style of classical Greek architecture.

Niche
Vertical hollow — or ornamental recess — in a wall originally designed to hold a small statue.

Nimbus
A halo.

Nineteenth-century see Greek Revival, Victorian.

Ninth-century see Saxon

Nogging
Brickwork (where only this is used) between the timber framework of a building.

Niche

Nook shaft
Pillar set in the right angle formed by adjoining vertical faces in a door jamb or window.

Norman period
English building from *c* 1066 to *c* 1200. Impressive, massive buildings with a large variety of vigorous mouldings on arches and doorways. Arches were semicircular, vaults were barrel-roofed but towers were mostly square. Aisles were added later in the period. Norwich Cathedral is a good example.

Obelisk
Square or several-sided stone shaft. Often used as a memorial, marker or headstone.

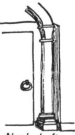
Nook shaft

Offset
Sloping part of a wall or buttress which has been exposed by a reduction in thickness of the section immediately above.

Ogee
Moulding shaped in a continuous, flowing, double curve which is concave above and convex below and springs from two opposing radii.

Ogee arch

Oratory
Private place of worship, built by a saint.

Order
Term used in classical architecture to define the entire structure which includes all parts of a column and the entablature. The five of these defined in classical architecture are Doric, Tuscan, Ionic, Corinthian and Composite. The last is a mixture of Ionic and Corinthian. Tuscan was a mixture of Doric and Composite which became a feature of Renaissance architecture. Doric, Ionic and Corinthian were the names which the Romans gave to the three types of column invented by the Greeks.

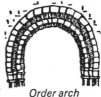
Order arch

Order arch
Receding arch of a doorway or window.

Ovolo
Convex moulding which runs either horizontally or along the contour of an arch in Renaissance architecture. The upper edge projects.

Parapet

Padstone
Stone block on the top of a wall between the beam which supports the rafters and the parallel timber which takes the ceiling laths or floorboards.

Painted glass see Stained glass

Palladian style
Architecture influenced by the designs of Andrea Palladio (1518-80), an Italian who was famous for his domestic buildings. Sir Christopher Wren modified this in much of his church-building and the style was copied by some of his successors in the same field.

Parapet spire

Parapet
Low wall above roof or eaves level of a tower or wall. It prevents accidents and breaks the visual line of a flat roof.

Parapet spire
A spire which rises wholly from within the parapet of a tower.

Parclose (screen)
Partition or screen around a shrine or chapel in order both to enclose it and to separate it from the main body of the church.

Pargetry
Plaster on exterior walls, sometimes decorated.

Parclose screen

Parish registers
Written records of christenings, marriages, burials, churchwarden's accounts, tithe books, etc. Originally kept in the parish chest; many are now in local authority's archives. First ordered to be kept in 1538.

Parvis
Enclosed area before the entrance to the church, or a room over the porch used as a schoolroom.

Pedestal

Paten
Flat cover for a chalice, which is also used to hold the sacred host.

Pellet moulding

Patera
Small circular or square decoration set at regular intervals in hollow moulding.

Pax
Tablet showing the Crucifixion which is kissed by both the priest and the congregation as a sign of peace.

Pedestal
Supporting base between a column and the plinth.

Pilaster

Pediment
Triangular upper frontage in Grecian style, featured in English Renaissance architecture; has the appearance of a low-pitched gable. Is used above doorways, windows, porticoes, etc.

PILLARS

Pellet moulding
Ornamental moulding of the Norman period, consisting of small spheres or beads in a continuous line.

Pendant
Hanging feature; especially applied to a boss in a medieval roof.

12th century   *13th century*

Perpendicular period
About 1350 to 1539. Church-building achieved its ultimate splendour in lofty proportions, vertical lines, large windows, high arches, traceried panels and decoration. Naves were large and aisles were wide. Battlemented parapets were joined by flying buttresses. The prosperity of wool merchants made so much of this possible.

Pew
Bench seat, often enclosed and with high walls and doors.

14th century   *15th century*

Pier
Vertical and freestanding pillar; cylindrical, octagonal, rectangular or in clusters. Mostly solid in construction except for those of the Norman period which were often filled with rubble. Usually ornamental, as well as a structural necessity.

Pilaster
Shallow rectangular column attached to, and projecting from, a wall on which it was used as a form of decoration. A feature of Saxon building.

early 13th century

Pillar
Vertical member, usually freestanding and supporting an arch. May also be attached to a wall as decoration.

Pillar and portico era
Term applied to the Classical age which lasted for about two hundred years from the mid seventeenth century and included the Baroque and Rococo styles.

13th century

Pillar piscina
Stone basin built on to a pillar or shaft, through which the water used by the priest was drained.

Pinnacle
Vertical turret to be found at the head of buttresses, roofs, gables, towers, etc. The elongated, cone-shaped head is usually decorated by crockets or other foliated shapes and the whole tapers to a pointed apex which is known as a finial.

14th century

Piscina
Niche, containing a stone bowl or drain, which is usually built on to the wall of the chancel near an altar. The bowls are shallow, sometimes canopied and built within a canopy. Water drains from them on to the consecrated ground outside the walls of the church. Double piscinas were sometimes used—one for the washing of hands, and the other for the sacred vessels. A piscina without an altar usually denotes the former position of one.

14th century

Pitch
Slope of a roof in relation to the horizon.

Plank chest see Boarded chest

Plantain leaf
Flat, broad, sectional leaf used as decoration, especially on fonts made of Tournai marble.

15th century

43

Plate
Valuable items such as bowls, chalices, cups, flagons, dishes, patens, etc, which belong to the church and are invariably made out of precious metals.

Plate tracery
The earliest form of ornamental ribbing in the upper section of Gothic windows; simply openings pierced in the solid flat surface. The forerunner of bar tracery.

Plantain leaf

Plinth
Lowest projecting base member of a pedestal, column or wall.

Ploughshare vault
Vault skewed at an angle and away from its normal radius.

Plate tracery

Polygonal
Many-sided. Usually applied to the shape of a chapel, apse, or the east end of the church.

Polypod
Means several-legged. Usually applied to the type of font which consists of a bowl which is supported by a central stem but has several other shafts either attached as decoration or constructed as additional supports.

Plinth

Poppy head
Leaf-like or floral carving which forms the decorated terminal on a bench-end or choir stall.

Porch
Covered entrance built against the outside wall of the church to protect the south doorway.

Porch tower
Tower, or upper rooms built in a tower-like shape, subsequently raised on an existing porch.

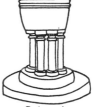
Polypod

Portico
Vertical columns set at regular intervals and supporting a roof. A form of porch, used in Classical styles.

Porticus
Loosely applied to a chapel or side chamber which abuts the main building, or a porch supported by a colonnade.

Poupee head
Alternative spelling of Poppy head.

Poppy head

Presbytery
Sanctuary reserved for the clergy and usually to be found beyond the choir at the east end of the church.

Priest's door
Small entrance for the use of the priest, usually located in the south wall of the chancel.

Principal rafter
Main rafter supporting the roof and taking the weight transmitted through the purlins.

Principal rafter

Processional cross
Ceremonial crucifix on a long stem, used to head processions.

Pulpit
Raised, fronted platform reached by steps and used by the preacher as a podium from which to deliver his sermons. Most are carved in wood; canopied Jacobean examples are very well done. There are rare stone pulpits.

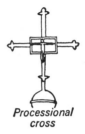

Processional cross

Pulpitum
Type of stone screen with a central doorway which — in a major church — divides the monk's quire from the rest of the building.

Purlin
Heavy horizontal beam which is set at a distance along the slope of a roof in order to conduct the weight from the common rafters to the principals.

Putlog hole
Square aperture which once held scaffolding.

Pulpit

Pyx
Vessel used to contain the consecrated bread used at the blessed sacrament.

Quadripartite vault
Vault which is divided into four sections of equal size by transverse diagonal ribs which cross at the centre.

Quarry
Diamond-shaped pieces of glass used in lattice windows.

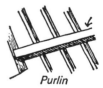

Purlin

Quatrefoil
Open tracery shaped as a four-lobed flower.

Queen Anne architecture see Hanoverian

Quatrefoil

Queen post
Vertical beam which joins the main rafters of a roof with the horizontal tie beam.

Quire
Alternative spelling of Choir.

Quirk
Sharp groove in the moulding immediately above or below a chamfer.

Queen post

Quoin
Large, dressed corner-stone as it forms the external angle at the meeting of two wall surfaces.

Quirk

Rabbet
Stepped semi-groove which is cut to project along the outer edge of a plank and exactly fit the groove in an adjoining plank.

Radiating chapels
Chapels built outwards in radial fashion from the wall at the east end of the church.

Rafter
The sloping beam in a timber roof which connects the ridge above with the wall plate. Several of these form the interior framework of the roof and support the boarding and the exterior covering.

Quoins

Rail
Horizontal member which connects a series of panels.

Reading desk see Lectern

Recessed grave
Burial chamber constructed within a thick wall.

Rectangle see Single-celled plan

Radiating chapels (plan)

Rectilinear
Characteristic straight-line, upright appearance of windows or panelling in the Perpendicular period.

Reformation
The religious revolution of the sixteenth century. It repudiated the supremacy of the Pope and resulted in the Protestant or Reformed church. There was some church-building, but generally very little until the eighteenth century.

Registers see Parish registers

Rafters

46

Renaissance period
Italian influence in English church architecture from 1485 to 1689, which formed the period between the Middle Ages and the Reformation.

Rere arch
Inner arch of a window or doorway which differs from the outer side.

Reredos

Reredos
Decorated screen or wall-covering behind the altar. May be a tapestry, painting, or a stone construction beneath the east window so shaped to accommodate figures of the twelve apostles.

Respond
Half pillar which is built against the wall at the end of an arcade.

Restoration
Rebuilding or repair of a potentially ruinous building. The term is often used in connection with the unaesthetical rebuilding by Victorian architects.

Respond

Retable
Raised shelf behind the altar, which sometimes takes the form of a decorated stone screen or panels. It is used to hold ornaments, candlesticks and vases.

Reticulated tracery
Form of pattern in tracery which consists of circles which are elongated into ogee shapes and repeated in a honeycomb pattern.

Retriculated tracery

Retro-choir
Section of a cathedral or a major church to the east of the choir, and behind any presbytery.

Rib
Arched — and generally moulded — member which supports a vault or ceiling and divides it into compartments.

Riddells
Curtains at the side of the altar.

Ribs

Ridge piece
Horizontal beam along the line where the sloping sides of a roof meet.

Ring of an arch
Plain or moulded right-angled contour of an arch.

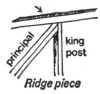

Ridge piece

47

Rococo
Successor to Baroque. Flamboyant style of European
architecture which originated in France in the mid
eighteenth century. Has since given its name to any
extremely ornamental style.

Roll moulding
Cylindrical or convex form of contour.

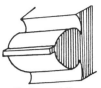

Roll moulding

Roll-top tomb see Bale tomb

Romanesque
Round-arched style of Saxon building. It became
typical of Norman work, with which it is most usually
associated.

Rood
The cross of Christ; symbol of the Christian faith.

Rood beam
Horizontal member which spans the chancel and
supports the rood above.

Rood loft
Gallery on top of the rood screen, usually carved and
supporting a large cross. Some still have statues of
Saint John and the Virgin. Such galleries were used
as access to the rood in order to clean and decorate it,
but many were destroyed at the Reformation.

Romanesque

Rood screen
Carved wooden or stone screen which divides the
nave from the choir and chancel. The rood was
placed over the screen.

Rood stairs
Steps leading to the rood loft, often through a pillar.

*Rood and
rood beam*

Roof truss see Truss

Rose window
Circular window with tracery radiating from the
centre.

Royal arms
Board or canvas square containing a painting of the
royal arms. They became a compulsory part of the
parish church after the Reformation.

*Rood loft and
rood screen*

Rubble
Rough infilling and stone fragments used in Norman
pillars, etc.

Rose window

Rubblestone
Unsquared, roughly hewn stones which have been irregularly constructed.

Rubble

Running vine
Decoration of the Decorated and Perpendicular periods, which takes the form of a continuous single vine with leaves falling alternately above and below the stem.

Running vine

Rusticated
Pitted, roughened surface to masonry.

Sacristy
Depository for the valuables owned by the church, such as the sacred vessels, vestments, etc.

Saddleback roof
Tower roof built in the shape of two opposite gables.

Saddleback roof

Saltire cross
Diagonal form in the shape of Saint Andrew's cross.

Sanctuary
Area to the east of the main altar rails, which includes the altar.

Sanctuary chair
Seat within the main altar rails, reserved for use by a visiting bishop. Many elaborately carved Jacobean examples remain.

double saddleback roof

Sanctuary ring
Knocker on the exterior door of the church. It was used by persons who wished to claim the ancient right of sanctuary within the building or churchyard, until they could be lawfully brought to trial.

Saltire cross

Sanctus bell
Small bell hung on the exterior of the church, usually in its own turret at the junction of the nave and the chancel. The bell is rung at the elevation of the host.

Saxon period
About 600 to 1066. Simple, single or two-celled buildings with the entrance at the west; often in wood, but later in stone. Complete churches of this period survive at Bradford on Avon, Wiltshire, and Escomb, County Durham.

Sanctus bell

Scalloped capital
Romanesque-style head to a column or pilaster — cube-shaped with the lower angles carved into a

4

series of cone shapes which are rounded towards the lower edge in order to meet the circular supporting shaft.

Scantling
Small beam.

Scissor beam

Scissor beam
Timber placed diagonally to its fellow from each side of a timber roof, so that at some point they cross through each other forming an X shape.

Scoinson see Rere arch

Scratch dial
Sundial which was lightly incised into the exterior wall of the church in order to tell the time for masses.

Sedilia,
13th century

Screen
Any partition which separates one part of the church from another. See also Rood screen, Jube.

Scribing
Cutting a moulding in order to meet it exactly at an angle.

Scuncheon arch see Rere arch

Sedilia
Set of two, three or four seats recessed in niches in the south wall of the chancel. Used by the priest and his assistants. Sedilia are often stepped, decorated and canopied and built in stone — although there are some wooden ones.

Sedilia,
14th century

See
Ecclesiastical extent of a bishopric.

Setback buttresses
Exterior supports placed an equal distance apart from the angle formed where two walls meet.

Set off see Offset

Seven sacraments fonts
Group of fifteenth and sixteenth-century fonts (almost exclusive to East Anglia) on which are carved illustrations of Baptism, Confirmation, Holy Eucharist, Penance, Extreme Unction, Holy Orders and Matrimony — although not necessarily in that order.

Seventeenth-century see Tudor, Elizabethan, Jacobean, Renaissance

Setback
buttress

Seventh-century see Saxon

Sexpartite vault
Four-sectioned (quadripartite) vault with an additional arch rib dividing it into six unequal parts.

Sgraffito
Decorated plasterwork.

Shaft
Any independent column, or the part of a pillar or column between the base and the capital.

Sexpartite vault (plan)

Shaft ring see Annulet

Shingle
Rectangular, wooden roofing or walling tile with one end thicker than the other.

Soffit

Shrine
Usually the tomb, altar or special chapel associated with a saint or martyr.

Single-celled plan
Earliest style of church-building in which there was no division between the nave and the chancel.

Single-framed roof
System of rafters, etc, in cross-section not joined along its length.

Sixteenth-century see Perpendicular, Tudor, Elizabethan, Renaissance

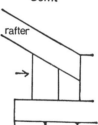
Sole piece

Sleeper
Large wooden post set into the whole height of a wall to support indirectly the timbers of the roof.

Soffit
Flat ceiling under a gallery, rood loft, etc. Otherwise the underside of an arch.

Sole piece
Timber placed on the top of a wall in order to provide a base for a rafter.

Sounding board

Sound hole
Opening pierced in a belfry wall for ventilation.

Sounding board
Horizontal canopy above a pulpit.

Spandrel
Space between two arches, or the triangular-shaped

Spandrel

51

blocking between the posts and beams of screens, roofs, etc. Sometimes decorated.

Spire
Tall, conical structure tapering to a point and built on top of a tower.

Squinch

Spire light
Pierced opening on the flat surface of a spire. It contains horizontal, ornamental stone openwork.

SPIRE SHAPES

Splay
Shape of masonry which slopes backwards towards a deep-set window in a thick wall.

Splay-foot spire
Type of broach spire with the broaches flattened outwards.

flat cap

Springer
Single block of stone in a wall from which springs the curve of an arch or the rib of a vault.

Squinch
Arches which are built across the interior angles of a square tower in order to support an octagonal superstructure.

blunt cap within the parapet

Squint see Hagioscope

Stained glass
Painted pieces of glass which, when held together by a lead-work frame, form a complete picture. The result is bound by the tracery of a window, and collectively often forms scenes of detail and beauty to be read right across the window.

pyramidal cap

Stair turret
Covered stairway which is built on the outside of the tower and gives access to the interior. Although some actually rise above the tower, most only reach the belfry stage.

overhanging cap

Stall
Fixed wooden seat in the chancel or choir; often carved or canopied.

Staple
Thin, curved piece of metal which was driven into the upper side of a font in order to secure the font cover. Such action was necessary in the Middle Ages because holy water was often left for very long periods, if it was not otherwise stolen for profane use.

short timber and shingle splay

52

Stave
Staff belonging to the churchwarden as guardian of the church, and often exhibited in the nave.

Steeple
The whole structure of a spire built on to a tower or roof where the two are not clearly defined into separate parts.

Stellar see Lierne rib

Stiff leaf
Early English decoration which resembles stiff stalks of curling leaves and is to be found on capitals, corbels, mouldings, bosses, etc.

Stoup
Stone basin used to hold holy water. Located inside the church or on the right-hand side of the porch.

Strainer arch
Arch which is built between two pillars in order to stabilise the structure.

String course
Projecting band of masonry running horizontally around the exterior of the church as well as between each stage of a tower.

Strut
Diagonal or upright brace, placed between the king post and the beam it supports in a wooden roof.

Stair turret

*Stiff leaf
(various forms)*

Stoup

pierced spire

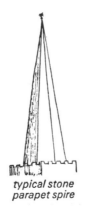
*typical stone
parapet spire*

spirelet

SPIRE SHAPES

53

Stucco
Decorative plasterwork.

Stud
Vertical piece of timber.

Superimpose
Formation of two layers of carving into a canopy.

Table tomb

Tabernacling
Covered, ornamental canopy of Gothic origin placed over an altar, choir stalls, etc.

Table tomb
Grave made of masonry in the shape of an altar, and raised above the level of the ground.

Tenon

Tenon
Projecting end of a piece of timber so prepared to fit into a mortise or socket.

Tenth-century see Saxon

Tester
Canopy above a pulpit.

Thirteenth-century see Early English, Decorated

Three-celled plan
Style of design which originated in the twelfth century, and consisted of nave, choir and sanctuary.

Three-decker pulpit
Accommodation ascending vertically in three tiers for the use of the clerk, the reader and the preacher. High box pews of the seventeenth and eighteenth centuries meant that the preacher had to be high off the ground to be seen by the congregation.

Three-decker pulpit

Tie beam
Large, horizontal main beam in a timber roof. It spans the distance between two walls and supports the rafters it connects on both sides.

Tie beam

Tierceron ribs
Subsidiary pairs of ribs which begin at the same point as the main supports but meet at an angle and do not complete a continuous line across the vault. They do not cross through the centre.

Tierceron vault
One containing ribs of the same name.

Tomb
Vault or grave containing human remains.

Tower (square type, Norman)

Tomb railings
Decorative metalwork used to enclose table tombs, or an altar in the fourteenth century.

Tombstone
Monumental stone, marble, etc. which denotes the position of a grave and often contains some biographical details of the deceased.

Tournai fonts
Large, richly decorated group of fonts made from blue-black marble taken from the quarries at Tournai on the Scheldt river in Belgium.

*octagonal type
(Early English)*

Tower
Square or circular structure rising above the roof of the church and usually positioned either centrally, at the crossing of nave and transepts, or at the west end. Some are detached from the main building.

Tower church see Turriform

Tracery
Perforated, ornamental stonework in a window, screen, panelling, etc.

round type

Transept
One arm of the crossing in a cruciform church.

Transitional period
Late Norman work from 1150 to 1200.

Transom
Horizontal cross-bar in wood or stone which spans a window, the top of a door, or is present in the tracery of a screen.

*central type
(14th century)*

*square type
(Early English)*

*square type
(Decorated)*

*square type
(Perpendicular)*

TOWERS

Transverse arch
Arch set at right angles to the axis of a vault which it divides into bays.

Trefoil
Foliated, three-lobed ornamentation in a pierced circle or at the head of an arch.

Trellis ornament
Norman decoration consisting of a continuous band of lattice work.

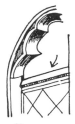

Transom

Tribune
Raised floor or gallery over an aisle, which has arched openings into the nave.

Triforium
Blank arcading, gallery or wall passage between the top of the main arcade and the clerestory above.

Triglyph
Decorative tablet in a frieze of classical ornamentation.

Transverse arches

Triptych
Three adjacent hinged panels of illustration or carving.

Truss
Rigid beam which supports rafters.

Trefoil

Tub font
Stemless, bucket-shaped font of Saxon and Norman periods.

Tudor period
Late Perpendicular period *c* 1485 to 1603, influenced by Renaissance styles.

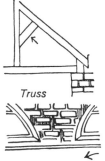

Truss

Tunnel vault see Barrel vault

Turriform
The complete church building including the tower as an integral part.

Tuscan see Order

Twelfth-century see Norman, Transitional, Early English.

Twentieth-century
Use of modern materials and simple designs to

Triforium

produce functional rather than decorative interiors and striking exteriors.

Two-celled plan
Eleventh-century style of building, dividing the church into nave and chancel.

Two-celled plan

Tympanum
Space between the lintel at the top of a doorway and the arch shape above it. Characteristic of Norman and Gothic building; the remaining examples often contain a sculpture in relief.

Undercroft
Underground crypt below a church.

Vault
Underground room of interment.

Tympanum

Vaulting
Arched roof, ceiling or arch-like structures with ribs radiating from a central point. See also Fan vaulting; Groined vault; Lierne vault; Quadripartite vault; Sexpartite vault; Tierceron vault.

Vesica
Pointed oval shape formed by the intersection of two circles of equal diameter.

Vestments
Clothes of office worn by the clergy, choristers, etc.

Vestry
Room within or adjoining the church and used by the priest to store vestments and items relevant to church matters.

Vesica

Vice
Spiral staircase winding around a pillar.

Victorian period
Time of nineteenth-century Gothic revival and terrible destruction under the guise of restoration.

Volute
Spiral twist of an Ionic capital, often to be found in Norman work.

Votive cross
Lightly scratched marking made as tangible proof of a personal vow.

Volute forms

Voussoir
Wedge-shaped stone block which, with others, makes up an arch.

Wagon roof
Curved roof with similarly shaped wooden rafters, together resembling the interior of a covered wagon. A feature of churches in Cornwall.

Wagon vault see Barrel vault

Wainscot
Panelled woodwork around the lower walls of the church, or in a similar position in wooden screens.

Wall arcade see Blind arcade

Wall painting
Any form of painted decoration within the church. May be whole scenes from the Bible, or repetitive or isolated two-dimensional representations of carved motifs (see also Doom painting).

Wall plate
Horizontal piece of timber which is placed on the top of either side of a wall in order to support the load imposed upon it by one of the rafters in the roof above.

Wall post
Vertical member which is placed against a wall in order to support the downward thrust of the roof.

Wall tablet
Commemorative plaque placed on the interior wall of the church. Contains biographical details of an individual or family, and sometimes an epitaph.

Water hold
Hollow between two cylindrical or convex mouldings at the base of a pillar

Waterleaf
Early English leaf-shape which begins in the centre of each face of a capital, divides outwards and curls upwards at its extremities towards the abacus.

Wattle and daub
Early wall which comprised a bound interweave of twigs and rods covered with mud and clay.

Weather boarding
A protective covering for an external wall surface,

Voussoir

Wagon roof

Wall post

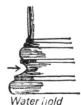
Water hold

Waterleaf

Saxon

Saxon

Norman

Norman

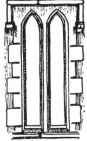

Early English

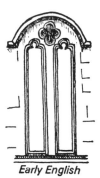

Early English

Early English

WINDOWS

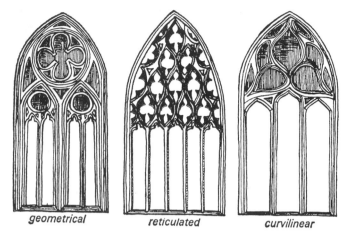

geometrical reticulated curvilinear

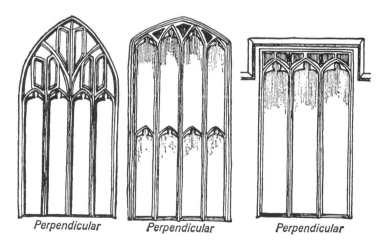

Perpendicular Perpendicular Perpendicular

WINDOWS

usually made of horizontal planks of wood which overlap each other.

Weather mould see Dripstone

Webbing
Filling between the ribs of a vault.

Weepers
Carved figures which are set in niches along the sides of a medieval tomb.

Weepers

Wheel window see Rose window

Wool church
Fine Perpendicular structure, built and enriched by the prosperity of the wool trade.

Yew tree
Usually found on the south side of the churchyard where yews were originally planted to protect the building from the elements. There was a pagan belief in its sacredness, and the tree later became a symbol of immortality. Its foliage was used as decoration at festivals.

Yew tree

Y-tracery
The resulting shape when a single mullion divides itself, forming an elongated diamond shape above two lights.

Y-tracery

Zigzag see Chevron

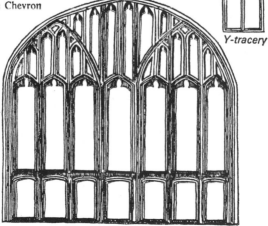
Window (Perpendicular)

Bibliography

Through several impressions of *Discovering Church Architecture* and its companion *Discovering Churchyards*, the original bibliographies have been updated. In recent years so many new books have been published on the subject that it is no longer possible to include them all, and it has become necessary to produce a more selective bibliography.

Church architecture has always been a subject to attract local researchers and writers and some of the best material over the last few years has been produced by private individuals, small publishers and societies on churches or particular features to be found in relatively small areas of the countryside. If you want to know what has been published on churches in your area, or on church architecture generally, you can consult the annual subject indexes to the British National Bibliography in your local library.

In the meantime, here is a selected general list.

Addison, W. *Local Styles of the English Parish Church*. Batsford, 1982.

Anderson, W. *The Rise of Gothic*. Hutchinson, 1985.

Atkinson, T. D. *Local Style in English Architecture*. Batsford, 1947.

Bailey, B. *Churchyards of England and Wales*. Hale, 1987.

Beaulah, K., and van Lemmen, Hans. *Church Tiles of the Nineteenth Century*. Shire, second edition forthcoming, 2001.

Betjeman, J. *Sir John Betjeman's Guide to English Parish Churches* (revised by N. Kerr). Harper Collins, 1993.

Blatch, M. *Parish Churches of England in Colour*. Blandford, 1974.

Bond, F. *Fonts and Font Covers*. Waterstone, 1985 reprint of 1908 edition.

Bowyer, J. *The Evolution of Church Building*. Crosby Lockwood, 1977.

Boyle, N. E. *Old Parish Churches and How to View Them*. Skeffington, 1951.

Brabbs, D. *English Country Churches*. Weidenfeld & Nicolson, 1985.

Bradley, Charles. *Let's Discover Churches* (children). Watts Books, 1993.

Braun, H. *Parish Churches: Their Architectural Development in England*. Faber, 1970.

Burgess, F. *English Churchyard Memorials*. Lutterworth Press, 1963.

Cave, C. J. P. *Roof Bosses in Medieval Churches*. Oxford University Press, 1948.

Chamberlin, E. R. *The English Parish Church*. Hodder & Stoughton, 1993.

Chapman, L. *Church Memorial Brasses and Brass Rubbing.* Shire, 1988; reprinted 1993.

Chatfield, M. *Churches the Victorians Forgot.* Moorland, revised edition 1989.

Child, M. *Discovering Churchyards.* Shire, 1982; reprinted 1989.

Child, M. *English Church Architecture: A Visual Guide.* Batsford, 1981.

Clapham, A. *English Romanesque Architecture.* Oxford University Press, 1934.

Clarke, B., and Betjeman, J. *English Churches.* Studio Vista.

Clifton-Taylor, A. *English Parish Churches as Works of Art.* Batsford, 1975.

Clowney, P. *Exploring Churches.* Lion, 1993.

Clucas, P. *England's Churches.* Colour Library Books, 1984.

Cocke, T. *Recording a Church.* Council for British Archaeology, 1982.

Cook, G. H. *The English Mediaeval Parish Church.* Phoenix, 1954.

Cook, G. H. *Mediaeval Chantries and Chantry Chapels.* Phoenix, 1947.

Cox, J. C. *English Church Fittings and Furniture.* Batsford.

Cox, J. C., and Ford, C. B. *Parish Churches of England.* Batsford, 1935.

Crossley, F. H. *English Church Craftsmanship.* Batsford, 1941.

Crossley, F. H. *English Church Design 1040-1540.* Batsford, 1945.

Crossley, F. H. *English Church Monuments.* Batsford.

Crossley, F. H. *English Church Woodwork and Furniture.* Batsford.

Curl, J. S. *Book of Victorian Churches.* Batsford, 1995.

Cunnington, P. *How Old is that Church?* Blandford, 1990.

Delderfield, E. R. *Ancient Churches for Beginners.* Raleigh Press.

Dirsztay, P. *Church Furnishings.* Routledge & Kegan Paul, 1978.

Durrant, G. M. *Landscape with Churches.* Museum Press, 1965.

Esdaile, K. A. *English Church Monuments 1510-1840.* Batsford, 1946.

Fisher, E. A. *Anglo-Saxon Towers.* David & Charles, 1969.

Fisher, E. A. *Greater Anglo-Saxon Churches.* Faber, 1962.

Greenoak, F. *God's Acre.* Orbis, 1985.

Hanna, M. *English Churches and Visitors.* English Tourist Board, 1984.

Harbison, R. *The Shell Guide to English Parish Churches.* Andre Deutsch, 1993.

Harries, J., and Hicks, C. *Discovering Stained Glass.* Shire, third edition 1996.

Harries, J. *Discovering Churches.* Shire, 1972; reprinted 1988.

Hayman, R. *Church Misericords and Bench Ends.* Shire, 1989; reprinted 2000.

BIBLIOGRAPHY

Howard, F. G. *Mediaeval Styles of the English Parish Church*. Batsford, 1936.

Howkins, C. *Discovering Church Furniture*. Shire, second edition 1980.

Hudson, K. *Churchyards and Cemeteries*. Bodley Head, 1984.

Hutton, G., and Smith, E. *English Parish Churches*. Thames & Hudson, 1952.

Jeffery, P. *The City Churches of Sir Christopher Wren*. Hambledon Press, 1996.

Jenkins, S. *England's Thousand Best Churches*. Allen Lane/Penguin Press, 1999.

Jones, L. E. *County Guide to English Churches*. Countryside, 1992.

Jones, L. E. *Enjoying Historic Churches*. Baker.

Jones, L. E. *Observer's Book of Old English Churches*. Warne, 1969.

Jones, L. E. *What to See in a Country Church*. Phoenix.

Kemp, B. *Church Monuments*. Shire, 1985; reprinted 1997.

Kemp, B. *English Church Monuments*. Batsford, 1981.

Kersting, A. F., and Vale, E. A. *Portrait of English Churches*. Batsford.

Laird, M. *English Misericords*. Murray, 1986.

Lindley, K. *Of Graves and Epitaphs*. Hutchinson, 1965.

Needham, A. *How to Study an Old Church*. Batsford.

Norman, E. R. *The House of God: Church Architecture, Style and History*. Thames & Hudson, 1990.

Nye, T. M. *Parish Church Architecture*. Batsford, 1965.

Pevsner, N. *Buildings of England* series. Penguin.

Platt, C. *Parish Churches of Medieval England*. Secker & Warburg, 1981.

Pounds, N. *Church Fonts*. Shire, 1995.

Randall, G. *The English Parish Church*. Spring, 1988.

Rouse, E. C. *Medieval Wall Paintings*. Shire, 1991; reprinted 1996.

Sinden, D. *The English Country Church*. Sidgwick & Jackson, 1988.

Smith, E., and Cook, O. *British Churches*. Dutton Vista, 1964.

Taylor, H. M. and J. *Anglo-Saxon Architecture*. Cambridge University Press, 1965.

Tracy, C. *English Gothic Choir Stalls 1200-1400*. Boydell, 1990.

Vallance, A. *English Church Screens*. Batsford.

Vallance, A. *Old Crosses and Lychgates*. Batsford.

Weir, A. *Images of Lust*. Batsford, 1986.